LLEWELLYN'S

SHADOWSCAPES
COLORING BOOK

ADVENTURES IN THE WORLD OF MYTH

Llewellyn's Shadowscapes Coloring Book is a collection of artist Stephanie Pui-Mun Law's favorite drawings produced as colorable illustrations for relaxation and enjoyment. The creator of popular companion products *Shadowscapes Tarot* and the *Shadowscapes Calendar*, Stephanie combines mythological symbols and personal inspiration to create surreal scenes and evocative otherworlds.

Stephanie began her career as an illustrator for fantasy gaming companies and publishers, working on projects for Wizards of the Coast in Magic, White Wolf, Alderac Entertainment, LUNA Books, and Palazzo Editions. In 2004, she began working on the *Shadowscapes Tarot* for Llewellyn Worldwide, which led to the publication of several successful Shadowscapes projects. Stephanie is also known for Dreamscapes, a series of art technique books designed to let anyone embark on a fantastical adventure of drawing and painting. In addition to her publishing projects, Stephanie has exhibited original works in Seattle, San Francisco, Nashville, San Diego, and New York.

Finding inspiration in the natural beauty of her native California, Stephanie combines the effervescent energy of wilderness with the beauty of dreams in all of her work. Through potent combinations of fantastical visions, archetypal imagery, and the energetic movement of dance, Stephanie invites you to create each illustration anew, lending your own intuitive vision of nature's rhythm and flow. For further inspiration, visit Stephanie online at www.shadowscapes.com.

The Art of Observation.

"Anomolly"
Stephanie Pui-Mun Law

"Unity"

A Moment of Music

Wind Machine
2011

ERATO